C000277290

ONE FOOT UP AND ONE FOOT DOWN
AND THAT'S THE WAY TO —

LONDON
TOWN

FLOREAT · LONDINIUM

COME CHILDREN ALL,
  BOTH GREAT AND SMALL,
  WITH EAGER EYE AND EAR,
  WHO DWELL AFAR OR NEAR
IN HOPE THAT SOME DAY YOU'LL CONTRIVE
TO VIEW GREAT LONDON'S BUSY HIVE,
AND HEAR THE MIGHTY HUM OF BEES
AT WORK ALIKE IN SUN OR SHOWER,
WHILE BUTTERFLIES BENEATH THE TREES
FLIT IDLY BY FROM FLOWER TO FLOWER
IN PARKS AND GARDENS BRIGHT AND GAY:
COME,—CLIMB SAINT PAUL'S WITH US TO-DAY,
  AND WITH THIS BOOK IN HAND,
  UPON THE DOME WE'LL STAND,
  AND THENCE LOOK DOWN
  O'ER LONDON TOWN.

# London Town

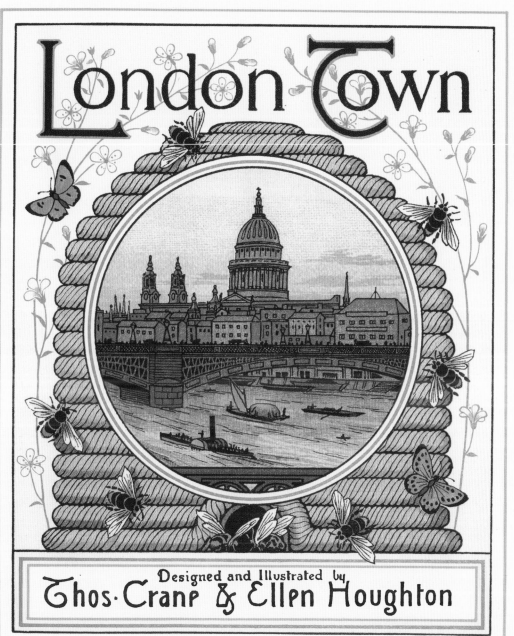

Designed and Illustrated by

## Thos. Crane & Ellen Houghton

LONDON

BELFAST · MARCUS · WARD · & · CO · NEW YORK

First published in 1883 by Marcus Ward & Co.

This edition published in 2011 by
The British Library
96 Euston Road
London NW1 2DB

©2011 The British Library Board

British Library Cataloguing in Publication Data
A catalogue record for this publication is available from
The British Library

ISBN 978 0 7123 5814 9

Cover design and additional typesetting by Andrew Shoolbred
Printed in Hong Kong by Great Wall Printing Co. Ltd

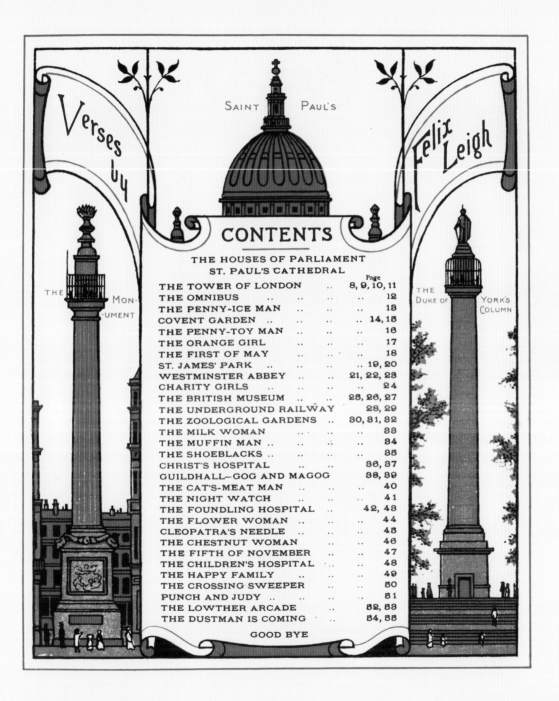

Verses by

Felix Leigh

SAINT PAUL'S

THE MONUMENT

THE DUKE OF YORK'S COLUMN

# CONTENTS

# The Tower of London

AMONG the sights of London Town
  Which little visitors wish to view,
The Tower stands first, and its great renown
  Has, you will notice, attracted Prue.

At a well-known spot, to Miss Prue's surprise,
  Some fine old ravens are strutting about.
If upon the picture a glance you cast,
  You will know the ravens next time, no doubt.

The red-coated guard who's watching here
  Is called a Beefeater—fancy that !
And Prue discovers, as she draws near,
  A child by his side who is round and fat.

"Father and Mother, pray come here,"
  In tones so pleasant, laughs lively Prue :
"You've shown *me* things that are odd and queer,
  A Beefeater's baby I'll show *you !*"

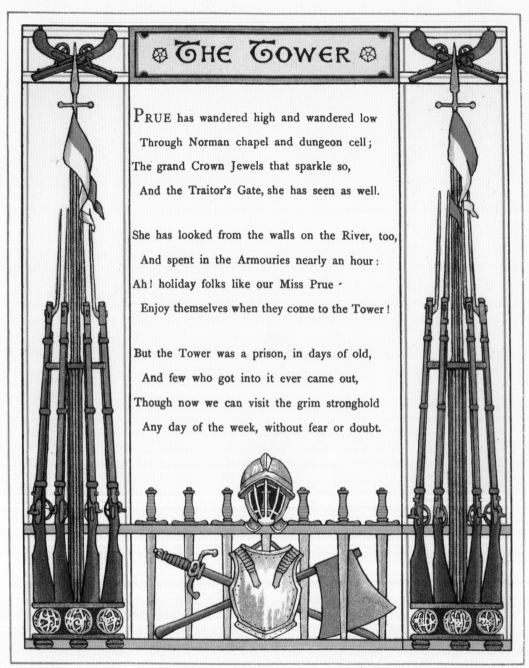

# THE TOWER

PRUE has wandered high and wandered low
  Through Norman chapel and dungeon cell;
The grand Crown Jewels that sparkle so,
  And the Traitor's Gate, she has seen as well.

She has looked from the walls on the River, too,
  And spent in the Armouries nearly an hour:
Ah! holiday folks like our Miss Prue -
  Enjoy themselves when they come to the Tower!

But the Tower was a prison, in days of old,
  And few who got into it ever came out,
Though now we can visit the grim stronghold
  Any day of the week, without fear or doubt.

# The Omnibus

EVERY day along the streets of mighty London Town

Nine hundred omnibuses rumble up and down.

When you're tired of walking, call " Hi! Conductor, stop!"

And he'll give you such a jolly ride, for twopence, on the top.

Sometimes by the 'bus's side small boys will run a mile,

Turning round just like the wheels, and hungry all the while:—

"We've not had any breakfast,—won't you toss us down a brown?"—

That's what they call a penny in the streets of London Town.

 # The Penny-Ice Man

IN summer when the sun is high,
　　And children's lips are parched and dry,
An ice is just the thing to try.
So this young man who comes, 'tis plain,
　　From Saffron Hill or Leather Lane,
A store of pence will quickly gain.
"A lemon ice for me," says Fred;
　　Cries Sue, "No, have a cream instead."
"A raspberry!" shouts Newsboy Ned.
"What fun!　Although we're now in June,
　　It feels"—says Ned—"this afternoon,
Like eating winter with a spoon!"

THIS is Covent Garden,
  What a lively scene!
Here are flowers so pretty,
  There are leaves so green.
These are busy buyers,
  Busy sellers those,
Selling, buying, selling,
  Everything that grows.

Fruits and lovely blossoms
  Hither come each day,
Fresh from *other* gardens
  Many miles away.
Cabbages potatoes,
  Pears and apples too,
Grapes, and pines, and peaches,
  All are here on view.

So the air is scented
  With the pleasant fruits,
With the bright-hued nosegays,
  And the springing roots.
For the little street-boys,
  Walking up and down,
It's almost like the country
  Brought to London Town.

# The Penny-Toy Man

"TOYS! toys! Penny Toys!
Toys for girls, and toys for boys!
Toys for dots who scarce can crawl,
Toys for youngsters stout and tall,
Toys for prince and peasant too,
Toys, my dears, for all of you!
Toys for girls and toys for boys!
Toys! toys! Penny Toys!"

That is how the toyman talks,
As through London Town he walks;
Bawling out his toyman's song,
While he slowly moves along,
On the pavement with a tray
Which is filled, from day to day,
With new toys to catch the eye
Of the youthful passer-by.

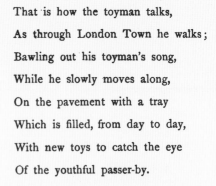

Sometimes it's a great big spider,
Like that Miss Muffet had beside her;
Sometimes it's a bat that flies,
Or a baby doll that cries;
Sometimes it's a frog that leaps,
Or a crocodile that creeps:
But whatever toy is shown,
For a penny it's your own.

# The Orange Girl

ORANGE-GIRL Kitty
  Here you may see.
That she is pretty
  All will agree.
"Three for a penny!"
  That is her cry;
No wonder many
  Hasten to buy.

Orange-girl Kitty
  Roams to and fro;
All through the city
  She's known high and low.
When the sun's shining,
  When the rain falls,
Never repining,—
  "Fine fruit!" Kitty calls.

Orange-girl Kitty's
  Mother, we're told,
Everyone pities—
  So feeble and old.
Poor mother's living
  Kitty obtains,
Cheerfully giving
  Her all that she gains.

# The First of May

CHIMNEY Sweeps' Day, Blackbird is gay,
Here he is singing, you see, in the "May."
He has feathers as black as a chimney sweep's coat,
So on Chimney Sweeps' Day he must pipe a glad note.

JACK IN THE GREEN

Jack-in-the-Green from door to door
Capers along with his followers four.
As May Day mummers are seldom seen,
Let us all give a copper to Jack-in-the-Green.

# St. James's Park

WHAT a countrified scene we have here!
Who would think London Town was so near,
That its murmur comes borne on the breeze
To the listener under the trees?

To this spot, to buy biscuits or buns,
Each city child joyously runs.
But the Park's greatest treat, they all vow,
Is a glass of new milk from the cow.

CRIED the drake to the ducks, "Here's a boy with a bun,
 Come, make haste! we shall have quite a feast!"
"Would you mind," said a swan, "if we shared in the fun?"
 "O dear no!" said he; "not in the least!"
It was surely through fear, not politeness at all,
 That the drake made so civil a speech,
For that one penny bun, after all, was so small,
 There was hardly a mouthful for each!


FROM the ducks and the swans on the lake, to next page—
 A much quieter scene—you may pass:
Though Westminster Cloisters are hoary with age,
 Yet green is their velvety grass,
And cheerily bright are their gables and peaks,
 As they glow in the westering sun:
'Tis some house in the Cloisters yon schoolboy seeks—
 Don't you wonder, now, which is the one?

The
Inner Cloisters
Westminster

## Westminster Abbey

IN all the land
A pile so grand
Is scarcely found
As this.  Around
Its old grey walls
The shadow falls
Of bygone years,
And so one fears
To raise one's tone,
When one is shown
Some ancient tomb,
Half hid in gloom.
Beneath such stones
There rest the bones
Of monarchs bold,
Whose story's told
For you and me
In history.

FROM kings of men
We wander; then
We're quickly brought
To kings of thought,
For poets lie
Interred hard by.
Here, too, repose
The bones of those
Who fought the foe
Long, long ago.
Brave knights were they;
And in the fray
They kept from shame
The English name,

And proved in fight
Great Britain's might.
Where they are laid
Their rest is made
As sweet as prayer
By music rare:
Over their head
The sleeping dead
Can daily hear
The anthem clear
Floating along
Like angel's song,
Until it dies
Like angel's sighs.

# On the way to the British Museum

NOT far from the British Museum there stands
  An apple stall, painted bright green,
Whence a penny may buy from the stall-keeper's hands
  Three apples, all rosy and clean.

    Now the girls of St. George's great Charity School
      Very often are passing that way,
    For their governors wise make this very good rule—
      They must go for a walk every day.

        How wistful the glances they cast as they pass,
          How they long for an apple to eat;
        But their pockets are quite without pennies, alas!
          To purchase so dainty a treat.

            These maidens have cheeks that are rosy and sweet
              As the choicest of fruit on the stall,
            And the very next time that we meet in this street,
              I'll buy apples enough for them all.

GOODNESS gracious! What a noise
   Baby Bunting's bent on making;
It is quite enough to set
   All the heads around him aching.
Still we're sure that Baby has
   Many griefs if we could see 'em,
For with other babes he's come
   Miles and miles to the Museum.
Baby Bunting thought, of course,
   When he said good bye to mother,
That he'd pass in through the gates
   With big sister and big brother.
But poor Baby finds, alas,
   That his little hopes have flitted,
For the nasty notice says
   "Babes in arms are not admitted."

BRITISH MUSEUM

BABIES IN ARMS
NOT ADMITTED

·In the British Museum·

NORTH WEST EDIFICE NIMROUD

# ·In the British Museum·

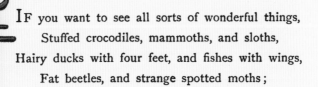

IF you want to see all sorts of wonderful things,
    Stuffed crocodiles, mammoths, and sloths,
Hairy ducks with four feet, and fishes with wings,
    Fat beetles, and strange spotted moths;

And enormous winged bulls with long beards, carved in stone,
    Dug up from Assyria's sand,
And old blackened mummies as dry as a bone,
    Discovered in Egypt's lone land,

And beautiful statues from Greece and from Rome,
    And other fine things without end,—
You will find you can see half the world here at home,
    If a day in this place you will spend.

# The Underground Railway

WHO is this in the Weighing Chair?
Why, little Dot, I do declare!
Three stone five! "So much as that?"
Calls out Miss Dot; "then I *must* be fat!"

On this and the opposite page you see
Dot's mother, and brother, and sisters three.
They wait for an underground train to come
And carry them swiftly back to their home.

Wonderful trains! From morn till night,
Clattering through tunnels without daylight,
Hither and thither they run, up and down,
Beneath the streets of London Town.

Many prefer these trains instead
Of the cabs and "Busses" overhead,
For they run much faster than horses can.
Miss Dot's papa is a busy man,

And goes to the City every day
By the "Underground,"--the quickest way:
And One Hundred Millions of people, 'tis found,
Are carried each year by the "Underground."

# The Zoological Gardens

AWAY we go to the famous Zoo'
  With Bertie, and Nellie, and Dick, and Sue.
And we feel quite ready to jump for glee
  When the wonderful birds and beasts we see.
The pelican solemn with monster beak,
  And the plump little penguin round and sleek,
Have set us laughing—Ha, ha! Ho! ho!
  And you'll laugh too, if you look below.
To the monkey-house then we make our way,
  Where the monkeys chatter, and climb, and play;
At the snakes we peep, then onward stroll,
  To talk to the parrots, and "scratch a poll."
And after all that, there will still be time
  On the patient elephant's back to climb.

# The Bear & the Buns

DON'T forget at the Zoo'
To take a good view
Of the funny old bear,
Who climbs out of his lair
Up a pole—Look, he's here,
With his figure so queer,
And his thick clumsy paws,
And his bun-seeking jaws.
On the end of a stick
Place a bun—"Now quick,
Master Bertie"—and, snap!—
What an awful red trap!—
The bun's out of sight,
But one more will delight
Father Bruin up there,
For his appetite's rare,
And he never says "No"
To a dozen or so.

# The Milk Woman

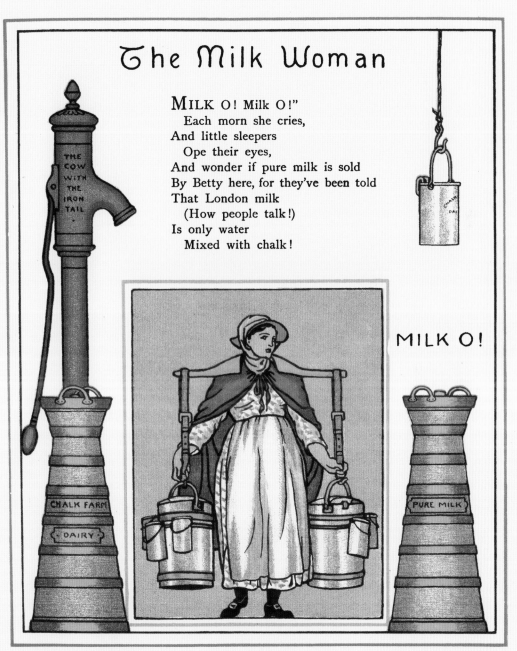

MILK O! Milk O!"
  Each morn she cries,
And little sleepers
  Ope their eyes,
And wonder if pure milk is sold
By Betty here, for they've been told
That London milk
  (How people talk!)
Is only water
  Mixed with chalk!

MILK O!

33

# The Muffin Man

YOU'VE heard about the muffin man,
 the muffin man, the muffin man,
You've heard about the muffin man
 who lives in Drury Lane?
Well, here you see that muffin man—
 that celebrated muffin man,
And if you try his muffins, you'll be sure to buy again.

MUFFINS

CRUMPETS

# The Shoeblack Brigade

IF you wanted a boy to polish your shoes,
Which of these two, do you think, you would choose?

They were once " Street Arabs," hungry, ill-clad,
And in very sore danger of going to the bad ;
But now !—one might think that their fortunes were made,
They're so proud to belong to the Shoeblack Brigade.

# The Blue-Coat Boys

IF you should pass through Newgate Street,
  Bareheaded boys with coats of blue,
Among the crowd you're sure to meet—
  And all with yellow stockings too.

Their coats are long as well as blue,
  And when at football they do play,
They find them rather heavy too,
  So tuck them up out of the way.

In Christchurch passage will be found
  The entrance to the School; and though
It looks so quiet, all around
  We hear the crowd go to and fro.

Above the doorway there you see
  The Boy King's statue:—Would you know
Who founded this great school? 'Twas he,
  More than three hundred years ago.

IN the famous Guildhall
Mayor and Alderman all
Meet to banquet and feast,
And it's whispered that they
Aren't inclined in the least
From the table to stray:
For they're fond of good cheer,
And they meet with it here,
Where the wine
Is so fine,
And still better than that,
Where the turtle's rich fat
Tempts the guests when they dine.
Turtle soup's very good,
And a favourite food,
With the banqueters all
Who frequent the Guildhall.

· GOG ·

38

Two giants so tall
Guard the famous Guildhall.
(Gog is one, and the other
Is Magog his brother.)
Well, these giants so tall
Watch the feast, but can't call
For a crumb,
As they're dumb,
And not living at all!
Else 'twould seem scarcely fair,
That when good things were by,
Gog and Magog should stare
From their pedestals high,
For if placed at a table
At least they'd look able,
To dine there and then
Like two live Aldermen!

MAGOG

# The Cat's-Meat Man

HE calls "Meat, meat!"
All down the street;
And dogs "bow-wow,"
And cats "mi-ow,"
While kittens sly
Come purring by,
As if to say—
"Do serve us, pray,
The first of all,
For we're so small."
The man throws bits
Of meat to kits,
And cats, and dogs;
Then on he jogs,
And down the street
Still cries "Meat, meat!"

PURVEYOR OF
CAT'S MEAT
TO HER MAJESTY

POLICEMAN A, Policeman B,

Likewise Policemen C and D—

All in a row, sedate and slow,

Away to their beats, tramp! tramp! they go.

# The
# Night Watch

Now the first is beloved by Ann the cook,

And his manly face has a bashful look,

As he thinks, with a sigh, of the beer and the pie

He has had from those area steps close by.

And here are three housemaids trim and slim;

Mr. B. knows Betty is fond of him;

But Policeman C loves Cicely,

And Dolly's engaged to Policeman D.

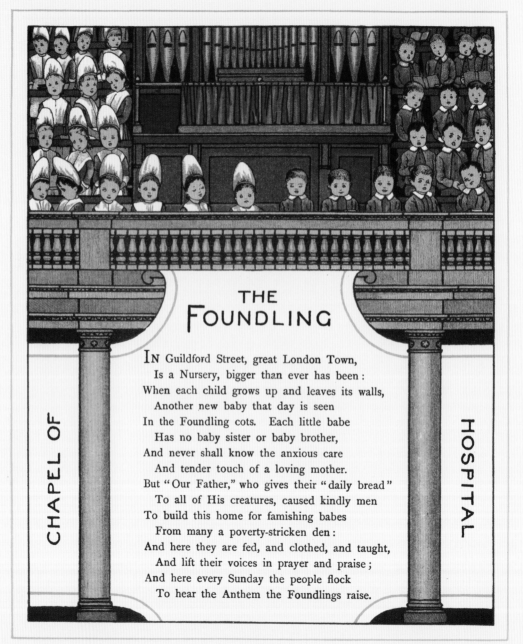

# THE
# FOUNDLING

CHAPEL OF

HOSPITAL

IN Guildford Street, great London Town,
  Is a Nursery, bigger than ever has been :
When each child grows up and leaves its walls,
  Another new baby that day is seen
In the Foundling cots.  Each little babe
  Has no baby sister or baby brother,
And never shall know the anxious care
  And tender touch of a loving mother.
But "Our Father," who gives their "daily bread"
  To all of His creatures, caused kindly men
To build this home for famishing babes
  From many a poverty-stricken den :
And here they are fed, and clothed, and taught,
  And lift their voices in prayer and praise ;
And here every Sunday the people flock
  To hear the Anthem the Foundlings raise.

AFTER CHAPEL,
See them all
Assembled in
The DINING HALL.

The bugle sounds
E'er grace is sung,—
Then fork and spoon
And lip and tongue

Clatter, chatter,—
*Such* a noise !
Oh ! such happy
.Girls and boys.

## The Flower Woman | ## Cleopatra's Needle

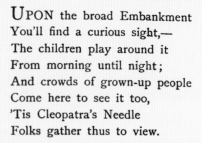

"FLOWERS sweet and fair, Sir,
　Flowers that any
Princess might wear, Sir—
　A bunch for a penny!"
Many a bunch
　Must the flower-woman sell,
To buy food for herself,
　And her children as well.

UPON the broad Embankment
You'll find a curious sight,—
The children play around it
From morning until night;
And crowds of grown-up people
Come here to see it too,
'Tis Cleopatra's Needle
Folks gather thus to view.

In Mother's pretty work-box
There's no such needle shown;
This needle, brought from Egypt,
Is nothing but a stone.
How silently it watches
Old Thames go gliding by!
"You're very old," the River says,
'But not so old as I."

Think you it longs for Egypt,
This wondrous solemn stone,
That stands and gazes at us
Each day so sad and lone?
Ah yes! when London's sleeping,
If monuments can dream,
It longs for Egypt's palm-trees,
And Nile's slow murmuring stream.

CLEOPATRA'S
NEEDLE

# The Chestnut Woman

"ALL hot! all hot! come buy!
  Ten a penny is the price,
And if you my chestnuts try,
  You'll declare they're very nice.
See how brightly burns my fire!
  Hear the chestnuts hiss and crack!
Better nuts you can't desire
  Than these beauties, big and black.

"All hot!—if you are cold,
  Have a pennyworth of heat,
Something nice and warm to hold,
  Something nice and warm to eat.
Munch your chestnuts up, and then,
  If your toes want warming too,
Say, 'I'll have another ten,
  Just to warm me through and through."

So the cheerful chestnut dame
  To each chilly passer calls,
As she roasts above the flame
  Fine round nuts like floury balls.
Hungry children soon draw near,
  If a penny they have got,
And with warmth and food to cheer,
  *They* become "all hot! all hot!"

# The 5th of November

THE fifth of November they bid you remember,
These bright little boys with the funny old Guy.
In his chair up and down he'll be borne through the town,
Then burned in a bonfire he'll be by-and-by.

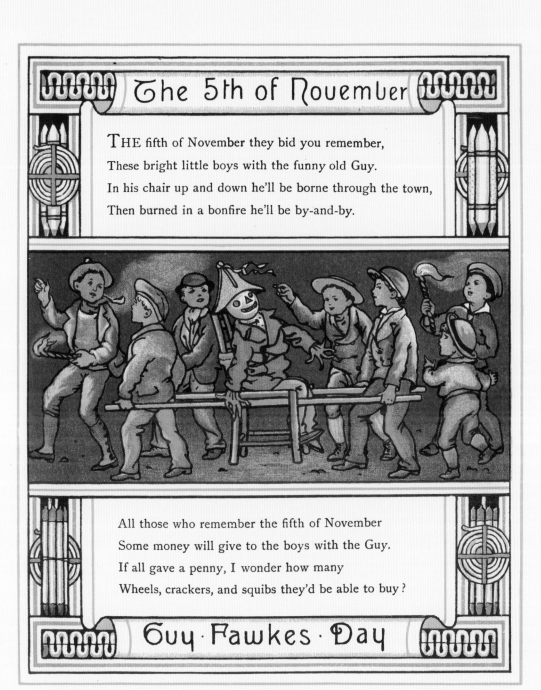

All those who remember the fifth of November
Some money will give to the boys with the Guy.
If all gave a penny, I wonder how many
Wheels, crackers, and squibs they'd be able to buy?

Guy · Fawkes · Day

# In the Children's Hospital

FEED MY LAMBS

LITTLE sick Tommy,
  What trouble he's had—
Medicine and blisters!
  His cough was *so* bad!

Now he is better:
  He soon will be well,
And go back to Mother,
  With stories to tell,

Of softly reclining
  On pillows of down,—
Of Mary his nurse
  In her pretty blue gown,

Of the doctor so gentle,
  The other sick boys,
And oh! a whole shopful
  Of beautiful toys!

# The Happy Family

HERE'S my Happy Family,
Little folks, as you may see:
Cats who fight, but just in fun,
Mice who up the flag-staff run,
Paroquet, canaries too,—

Now, my dears, 'twixt me and you,
Girls and boys who scold and tease,
Might a lesson learn from these
Birds and beasts who all agree
In my Happy Family.

# The Crossing Sweeper

HE is weak and old, and he feels the cold,
  But a nice clean path he keeps,
For passengers all, both great and small,
  As the mud to each side he sweeps.
The people stare, in London Town,
At his turban rare, and his face so brown,
But the poor old Hindoo does not mind,
So long as a coin for him they find.
And he nods and smiles, as he sweeps away,
As if to the passer-by he'd say,—
"Think of your shining boots and shoes,
And a copper to me you can't refuse.
For each penny I get I sweep the faster—
Ah! thank you,
        Thank you,
            Kind young master!"

# PUNCH · AND · JUDY

HAVE you a penny? well then, stay!
Haven't you any? don't go away!
Punch holds receptions all through the day,
Squeaking aloud to gather a crowd,
Scolding at Toby, beating his Wife,
Frightening the Constable out of his life,
And making jokes in a terrible passion,
As is Mr. Punch's peculiar fashion;
For this is his old, delightful plan
Of getting as many pence as he can.
    Then away he'll jog,
    With his Wife and his Dog,
    New folks to meet
    In the very next street.

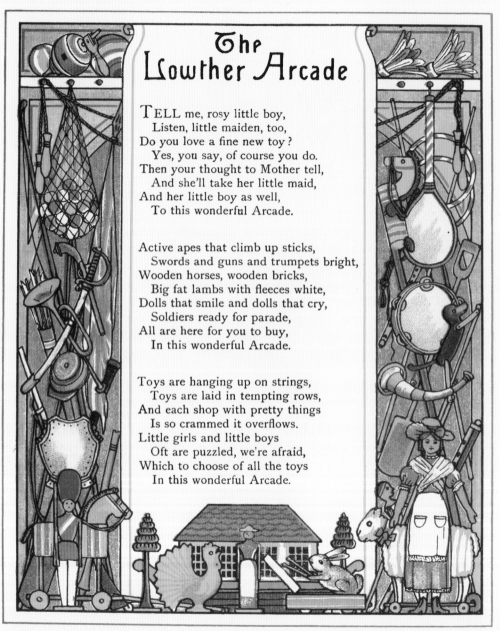

# The Lowther Arcade

TELL me, rosy little boy,
　Listen, little maiden, too,
Do you love a fine new toy?
　Yes, you say, of course you do.
Then your thought to Mother tell,
　And she'll take her little maid,
And her little boy as well,
　To this wonderful Arcade.

Active apes that climb up sticks,
　Swords and guns and trumpets bright,
Wooden horses, wooden bricks,
　Big fat lambs with fleeces white,
Dolls that smile and dolls that cry,
　Soldiers ready for parade,
All are here for you to buy,
　In this wonderful Arcade.

Toys are hanging up on strings,
　Toys are laid in tempting rows,
And each shop with pretty things
　Is so crammed it overflows.
Little girls and little boys
　Oft are puzzled, we're afraid,
Which to choose of all the toys
　In this wonderful Arcade.

# ·The Dustman is coming·

OFF to bed the pets must flock.
Look! it's nearly eight o'clock.

Baby's sleepy, so is Claire—
"Ah!" says Mother on the stair,
To little folks that yawn and blink,
"The dustman's coming, I should think."

Mother's right, for sure enough
Here's the dustman, strong and bluff.
"Dust ho! dust ho!" hear his cry,
As the dust-cart rumbles by.

The dustman home is going soon,
For there you see the rising moon.
And sleepy Claire, in cot so white,
Thinks that his cry must mean "Good Night."

# GOOD-BYE